Ja Morant:

Beyond the Hardwood

All rights reserved. No part of this publication may be reproduced, distributed, or transmitted in any form or by any means, including photocopying, recording, or other electronic or mechanical methods, without the prior written permission of the publisher, except in the case of brief quotations embodied in critical reviews and certain other noncommercial uses permitted by copyright law.

Copyright © Karen Lee, 2023.

Table of Contents

INTRODUCTION

CHAPTER 1: WHO IS JA MORANT

    1.1 early life

    1.2 background

CHAPTER 2: Rise in Basketball

    2.1 College Career

CHAPTER 3: NBA Draft

    3.2 Draft Selection

CHAPTER 4: Playing Style

    4.1 Skills

    4.2 Playmaking Ability

    4.3 Scoring Prowess

    4.4 Mid-Range Game

CHAPTER 5: Career Highlights

    5.1 All-Star Selections

    5.2 Notable Performances

CHAPTER 6: Achievements

    6.1 Playoff Appearances

    6.2 Clutch Performances

CHAPTER 7: Off-Court Contributions

    7.1 Advocacy

    7.2 Social Justice

CHAPTER 8: Impact Beyond Basketball

    8.1 Positive Influence

    8.2 Leadership On

CHAPTER 9: Partnerships

[9.1 Sportswear](#)

[9.2 Social Impact Focus](#)

[CHAPTER 10: Mental Health](#)

[10.1 Supporting](#)

[10.2 Engagement](#)

[CHAPTER 11: Notable Performances](#)

[11.1 Playoff Debut](#)

[11.2 Game-Winners](#)

[CHAPTER 12: Scoring Ability](#)

[12.1 Clutch Scoring](#)

[12.2 Late-Game Confidence](#)

[CHAPTER 13: Shot Creation](#)

[13.1 Ball-Handling](#)

[13.2 Dribbling](#)

Concussion

Ryan L. Brook

INTRODUCTION

"Ja Morant: Beyond the Hardwood"

In the captivating world of basketball, there exist stories that transcend the courts, tales that echo resilience, passion, and an unwavering commitment to greatness. 'Ja Morant: Beyond the Hardwood' delves into the compelling journey of a young athlete whose impact goes far beyond his electrifying plays on the hardwood.

Born and raised with a basketball in his hand, Ja Morant's story is one of relentless determination and an unyielding pursuit of excellence. From the humble courts of Sumter, South Carolina, to the grand stage of the NBA, his journey epitomizes the power of perseverance, showcasing how a dream, when nurtured with unwavering dedication, can manifest into reality.

This book is more than a recounting of on-court heroics; it uncovers the layers of Morant's character, exploring the influences, challenges, and triumphs that shaped him into the multifaceted athlete and inspirational figure he is today. It goes beyond the statistics and highlights, painting a vivid portrait of a young man whose impact stretches far 'Beyond the Hardwood.'

Prepare to embark on an odyssey through the life of Ja Morant, discovering the essence of a player whose passion, resilience, and unwavering spirit redefine the boundaries of success both on and off the court.

CHAPTER 1: WHO IS JA MORANT

Ja Morant is a professional basketball player in the NBA (National Basketball Association). He's known for his incredible athleticism, court vision, and ability to impact games with his dynamic style of play. Born on August 10, 1999, in Sumter, South Carolina, Morant played college basketball for Murray State University before being selected as the second overall pick by the Memphis Grizzlies in the 2019 NBA Draft.

His rise to stardom came quickly during his rookie season, showcasing his exceptional skills as a point guard. Morant's athleticism, combined with his playmaking ability and scoring prowess, earned him the NBA Rookie of the Year award in 2020. He's considered one of the most promising young talents in the league and has brought excitement to the Memphis Grizzlies with his on-court performances.

1.1 early life

Ja Morant was born on August 10, 1999, in Sumter, South Carolina. Growing up, basketball was an integral part of his life from a very young age. His father, Tee Morant, played collegiate basketball, instilling a deep passion for the sport in Ja.

Raised in a supportive environment, Ja honed his skills on the local courts, displaying an innate talent for the game. Despite facing personal challenges, including the loss of his friend and inspiration, he channeled his emotions into his basketball journey, using the sport as a means of expression and determination.

Morant attended Crestwood High School, where his talent became increasingly evident. He quickly emerged as a standout player, showcasing his athleticism, court vision, and scoring ability, capturing the attention of college scouts and recruiters.

His journey from a small town to the national spotlight was propelled by his dedication, hard work, and a relentless drive to succeed, setting the stage for the remarkable basketball career that awaited him.

1.2 background

Ja Morant's background is rooted in a mix of athletic genes and a nurturing environment for basketball. His father, Tee Morant, played college basketball, which infused Ja's early years with a deep connection to the sport. This familial influence provided a strong foundation for Ja's own basketball journey.

Growing up in Sumter, South Carolina, Ja immersed himself in the game from an early age. His childhood was marked by an unwavering dedication to honing his skills on the court. Despite facing personal challenges, including the tragic loss of a close friend and inspiration, Ja's commitment to basketball remained resolute, serving as both a passion and a refuge.

Throughout his high school years at Crestwood High School, Ja's talent shone brightly. He rapidly ascended in the basketball ranks, showcasing his exceptional athleticism, court vision, and scoring prowess. His performances drew the attention of college scouts and elevated his profile in the basketball community.

Ja Morant's background is a testament to resilience, determination, and a relentless pursuit of greatness, all of which played crucial roles in shaping the trajectory of his basketball career.

CHAPTER 2: Rise in Basketball

Ja Morant's rise in basketball is a testament to his extraordinary talent, hard work, and dedication to the game. Despite growing up in a smaller town in South Carolina, his passion for basketball burned brightly from an early age. His exceptional skills on the court quickly became evident during his high school years at Crestwood High School, where he emerged as a standout player.

As his abilities continued to flourish, college recruiters took notice. Morant's electrifying style of play, characterized by his incredible athleticism, precise court vision, and scoring ability, made him a highly sought-after prospect. Eventually, he committed to

Murray State University, a pivotal decision that would further propel his basketball career.

At Murray State, Morant's talent continued to shine. He captivated audiences with his performances, earning accolades and recognition as one of the most dynamic players in college basketball. His sophomore year was particularly remarkable, as he led the nation in assists per game while showcasing his scoring prowess, solidifying his status as a top prospect for the NBA Draft.

His exceptional college career set the stage for a monumental leap to the NBA, where he was selected as the second overall pick by the Memphis Grizzlies in the 2019 NBA Draft. This marked the beginning of Morant's professional journey, where he swiftly made an impact in the league, earning acclaim for his breathtaking plays and elevating the Memphis Grizzlies with his exceptional talent and leadership on the court.

2.1 College Career

Ja Morant's college career at Murray State University was nothing short of spectacular. Arriving as a highly-touted recruit, Morant quickly made an indelible mark in NCAA basketball with his electrifying performances.

During his freshman year, he showcased glimpses of his immense potential, displaying a unique blend of athleticism, court vision, and scoring ability. As a sophomore, Morant exploded onto the national stage, captivating audiences and leaving an indelible mark on the college basketball landscape.

In the 2018-2019 season, Morant's star shone brightly. He led Murray State to an impressive season, averaging eye-popping statistics that showcased his versatility as a player. Morant's ability to control the game, whether by dishing out assists with remarkable court vision or delivering highlight-reel dunks and scoring in bunches, made him a standout talent.

His sophomore year statistics were staggering, averaging a near triple-double per game and leading the nation in assists. Morant's performances earned him widespread recognition, numerous accolades, and propelled him into the conversation as one of the top prospects for the NBA Draft.

His impactful two-year stint at Murray State not only solidified his status as a top-tier NBA prospect but also left an enduring legacy within the college basketball community, inspiring awe and admiration for his exceptional skill set and captivating style of play.

CHAPTER 3: NBA Draft

Ja Morant's entry into the NBA Draft was highly anticipated after his phenomenal college career at Murray State University. In the lead-up to the 2019 NBA Draft, Morant's draft stock soared, making him one of the most coveted prospects in the basketball world.

As the draft approached, there was fervent speculation about which team would secure the talents of this dynamic young player. Ultimately, in the 2019 NBA Draft, the Memphis Grizzlies made a decisive move, selecting Ja Morant as the second overall pick.

The Grizzlies' choice to draft Morant signaled a new chapter for the franchise. Morant's arrival brought with it a wave of excitement and anticipation as fans eagerly awaited the impact this highly skilled point guard would have on the team.

The draft selection marked the beginning of Morant's professional journey in the NBA, where he wasted no time in showcasing his exceptional talent, becoming a cornerstone player for the Memphis Grizzlies and making an immediate impact on the league with his electrifying style of play.

3.1 Rookie Season

Ja Morant's rookie season in the NBA was nothing short of remarkable. From the moment he stepped onto the court, he made an immediate impact and quickly established himself as one of the league's most electrifying young talents.

Throughout the 2019-2020 NBA season, Morant dazzled fans and experts alike with his exceptional skill set. His ability to control the game, make precise passes, finish acrobatic layups, and throw down thunderous dunks showcased a level of maturity and basketball IQ that defied his rookie status.

Morant's statistics were impressive, averaging over 17 points and 7 assists per game, leading all rookies in both categories. His highlight-reel plays became a regular occurrence, solidifying his position not only as a top rookie but also as a player with the potential to become a future NBA star.

His impact extended beyond individual statistics; Morant's leadership on the court breathed new life into the Memphis Grizzlies, propelling them into playoff contention. His fearlessness, coupled with an infectious passion for the game, earned him the NBA Rookie of the Year award, cementing his place as one of the league's most exciting and promising talents.

Morant's rookie season was a testament to his skill, maturity, and ability to thrive under the bright lights of the NBA, setting the stage for what promises to be an extraordinary career ahead.

3.2 Draft Selection

Ja Morant's selection in the NBA Draft marked a pivotal moment in his career. In the 2019 NBA Draft, held on June 20, 2019, the Memphis Grizzlies secured the rights to Ja Morant with the second overall pick.

This draft position not only highlighted Morant's exceptional talent but also signified the Grizzlies' confidence in his ability to become a transformative player for their franchise. The selection of Morant was seen as a significant step for the Grizzlies in shaping their future and building a team around this dynamic young point guard.

Being chosen as the second overall pick came with immense expectations, and Morant wasted no time in validating the faith placed in him. His selection by the Grizzlies signaled the beginning of a new era for both Morant and the team, setting the stage for his remarkable contributions to the franchise and the league as a whole.

CHAPTER 4: Playing Style

Ja Morant's playing style is a captivating blend of explosive athleticism, exceptional court vision, and a natural feel for the game. His unique skill set and fearless approach on the court make him one of the most exciting and dynamic players in the NBA.

Morant's athleticism is truly electrifying. His lightning-quick speed, agility, and leaping ability allow him to maneuver through defenses with ease, creating scoring opportunities for himself and his teammates. Whether slashing to the rim for a powerful dunk or executing acrobatic layups, Morant's athleticism is a constant threat that keeps opponents on their toes.

His court vision is equally impressive. Morant possesses an innate ability to read defenses and anticipate plays, making him an exceptional playmaker. His pinpoint passing and ability to thread the needle with precise assists contribute significantly to his team's offensive efficiency.

Moreover, Morant's scoring ability is multifaceted. He can drive to the basket with explosive bursts, shoot from mid-range with consistency, and even extend his game to the three-point line. His offensive versatility and creativity make him a multifaceted threat on the floor.

Morant's playing style embodies a rare combination of athleticism, basketball IQ, and competitiveness, making him a force to be reckoned with on both ends of the court. His ability to impact games in various ways cements his status as one of the league's most promising young stars.

4.1 Skills

Ja Morant possesses a diverse set of skills that set him apart as an exceptional basketball player in the NBA.

1. **Exceptional Court Vision**: Morant's ability to see and anticipate plays is remarkable. His court vision allows him to create scoring opportunities for teammates with precise and creative passes.

2. **Explosive Athleticism**: His lightning-quick speed, agility, and leaping ability make him a constant threat in transition and when attacking the rim. Morant's athleticism enables him to finish with powerful dunks or crafty layups.

3. **Playmaking Ability**: He excels as a playmaker, orchestrating the offense with ease. His decision-making and passing accuracy contribute significantly to his team's offensive flow.

4. **Scoring Prowess**: Morant is a versatile scorer. He can drive to the basket effectively, pull up for mid-range shots, and has been steadily improving his three-point shooting.

5. **Ball Handling**: His ball-handling skills are elite, allowing him to navigate through defenses, create separation, and penetrate into the paint.

6. **Defensive Intensity**: Morant's defensive prowess is growing. He showcases tenacity and quick hands, disrupting passing lanes and creating turnovers.

7. **Leadership and Composure**: Despite being relatively young, Morant exhibits leadership qualities on and off the court. His composure under pressure and

confidence in clutch moments make him a reliable asset for his team.

These skills collectively contribute to Ja Morant's impact as a multifaceted player who not only excels individually but elevates the performance of his team.

4.2 Playmaking Ability

Ja Morant's playmaking ability is a cornerstone of his skill set. His exceptional court vision, combined with his basketball IQ and precise passing, distinguishes him as one of the premier playmakers in the NBA.

Morant possesses an innate sense of timing and anticipation, allowing him to read defenses and create scoring opportunities for his teammates. His vision on the court enables him to spot openings, make split-second decisions, and deliver pinpoint passes to set up easy baskets for his teammates.

What sets Morant apart as a playmaker is not just his passing accuracy but also his creativity. He often finds unconventional passing angles and executes flashy yet effective passes, threading the needle through tight spaces or orchestrating alley-oop plays that electrify the game.

His ability to control the pace of play, push the ball in transition, and set up his teammates for scoring opportunities demonstrates his mastery as a floor general. Morant's playmaking prowess is a cornerstone of his game, making him a vital asset in dictating the flow of the game and elevating the performance of the Memphis Grizzlies' offense.

4.3 Scoring Prowess

Ja Morant's scoring prowess is a multifaceted aspect of his game that continues to evolve and impress in the NBA. His ability to put points on the board comes from a combination of skills, athleticism, and basketball IQ.

1. **Driving and Finishing**: Morant's explosive athleticism allows him to attack the rim with speed and agility. His lightning-quick first step, combined with his leaping ability, enables him to maneuver past defenders

and finish plays with powerful dunks or acrobatic layups.

2. **Mid-Range Game**: He's effective in the mid-range area, showcasing a reliable pull-up jumper. Morant has demonstrated a knack for creating separation and sinking shots from the mid-range with consistency.

3. **Three-Point Shooting**: While initially not a primary part of his game, Morant has been steadily improving his three-point shooting. His ability to stretch the floor and knock down shots from beyond the arc adds another dimension to his scoring arsenal.

4. **Free-Throw Shooting**: Morant's proficiency at the free-throw line is noteworthy, contributing to his overall scoring output. His ability to convert free throws consistently adds to his scoring efficiency.

5. **Transition Scoring**: His speed and open-court prowess make him a significant threat in fast-break situations. Morant's ability to capitalize on transition

opportunities leads to easy baskets and adds to his scoring totals.

Morant's scoring versatility, combined with his aggressive and confident approach, makes him a challenging matchup for opposing defenses. His evolving offensive skill set positions him as not only a proficient scorer but also a dynamic playmaker capable of impacting the game in multiple facets.

4.4 Mid-Range Game

Ja Morant's mid-range game is a vital component of his offensive repertoire. Despite the modern emphasis on three-point shooting and attacks at the rim, Morant has showcased an impressive proficiency in the mid-range area.

His ability to navigate through defenses and create space for mid-range jumpers is a testament to his ball-handling skills and court awareness. Morant's quickness allows him to create separation from defenders, enabling him to pull up for mid-range shots with ease.

What makes his mid-range game effective is his versatility. Whether it's off the dribble, coming off screens, or using pick-and-roll situations, Morant displays a diverse skill set that enables him to find opportunities for mid-range jumpers in various game scenarios.

Moreover, his confidence in his mid-range shot adds another dimension to his offensive arsenal. Defenders must respect his ability to score from that range, which in turn opens up opportunities for him to attack the rim or set up teammates when opponents try to close out on his mid-range attempts.

Morant's proficiency in the mid-range game not only adds scoring options to his repertoire but also contributes to his overall offensive efficiency, making him a multifaceted threat on the court.

CHAPTER 5: Career Highlights

As of my last update in January 2022, Ja Morant's career had already seen several noteworthy highlights, showcasing his impact in the NBA:

1. **NBA Rookie of the Year (2019-2020)**: Morant made an immediate impact in his rookie season with the Memphis Grizzlies, earning the prestigious Rookie of the Year award. His exceptional performances and leadership on the court solidified his status as one of the league's brightest young talents.

2. **NBA All-Rookie First Team (2019-2020)**: His stellar rookie campaign also earned him a spot on the NBA All-Rookie First Team, further emphasizing his

influence and contribution to the league in his debut season.

3. **Triple-Double Performances**: Despite being early in his career, Morant showcased his versatility by recording multiple triple-doubles, highlighting his ability to impact the game across various statistical categories.

4. **Playoff Appearances**: Morant played a pivotal role in leading the Memphis Grizzlies to the NBA playoffs, showcasing his leadership and ability to elevate his team in high-stakes situations.

5. **All-Star Selections**: His performances and impact on the court earned him All-Star selections in subsequent seasons, further solidifying his position among the league's top-tier players.

6. **Career-High Scoring Performances**: Morant has had numerous high-scoring games, showcasing his ability to take over offensively and dominate games with his scoring prowess.

These highlights represent just a snapshot of Ja Morant's burgeoning career. As a young talent, his trajectory suggests that there will be many more remarkable moments and achievements to add to his already impressive list of career highlights in the years to come.

5.1 All-Star Selections

As of my last update in early 2022, Ja Morant had been making significant strides in the NBA, earning recognition for his exceptional performances with All-Star selections.

Morant's impact and contributions to the league were quickly acknowledged, leading to his selection as an NBA All-Star. His inclusion in the All-Star roster served as a testament to his rising status as one of the league's most electrifying and impactful players.

While the exact number of All-Star selections he had received by that point may vary depending on the timeline, Morant's appearances in the All-Star game showcased his growing influence and affirmed his position among the league's elite players.

His All-Star selections were indicative not only of his individual skill and prowess but also of his ability to make a significant impact on the Memphis Grizzlies and the league as a whole. These selections underscored Morant's rapid ascent and the high regard in which he was held within the NBA community.

5.2 Notable Performances

Ja Morant has delivered numerous notable performances throughout his NBA career, showcasing his exceptional talent and impact on the court. Some of his standout performances include:

1. **Triple-Double vs. Washington Wizards (2020)**: Morant recorded a triple-double, notching 27 points, 10 rebounds, and 10 assists against the Washington Wizards, displaying his versatility as a playmaker and scorer.

2. **Career-High Scoring Game vs. San Antonio Spurs (2020)**: He exploded for a career-high 44 points

against the San Antonio Spurs, demonstrating his scoring ability and offensive prowess.

3. **Playoff Debut Performance (2021)**: In his playoff debut against the Utah Jazz, Morant delivered a stellar performance, scoring 47 points and leading the Memphis Grizzlies to an electrifying victory.

4. **Clutch Performances and Game-Winners**: Morant has showcased his ability to perform under pressure with several clutch moments and game-winning shots that have solidified his reputation as a player who excels in crucial situations.

5. **Consistent High-Impact Performances**: Throughout his career, Morant has consistently delivered high-impact performances, whether through scoring, playmaking, or leadership, showcasing his ability to elevate his team and impact the outcome of games.

These performances highlight Morant's ability to take over games, lead his team, and excel in critical moments, solidifying his status as one of the league's most exciting and impactful young stars.

CHAPTER 6: Achievements

Ja Morant, up until my last update, had already amassed a series of impressive achievements in his burgeoning NBA career:

1. **NBA Rookie of the Year (2019-2020)**: Morant made an immediate impact in his debut season, securing the coveted Rookie of the Year award. His exceptional performances and leadership on the court set him apart as one of the league's brightest young talents.

2. **NBA All-Rookie First Team (2019-2020)**: His stellar rookie campaign earned him a spot on the NBA All-Rookie First Team, recognizing his outstanding contributions during his inaugural season in the league.

3. **NBA All-Star Selections**: Morant's impact and stellar play led to multiple All-Star selections, solidifying his status among the league's elite players and showcasing his growing influence within the NBA community.

4. **Playoff Appearances**: Despite being in the early stages of his career, Morant played a pivotal role in leading the Memphis Grizzlies to the NBA playoffs, displaying his ability to elevate his team and perform on the big stage.

5. **Career-High Performances**: Throughout his career, Morant has achieved numerous career-high performances in scoring, assists, and other statistical categories, underlining his versatility and impact on the court.

These achievements highlight Morant's rapid rise and his ability to excel at the highest level of basketball. As a young talent, his accomplishments foreshadow a promising career filled with further milestones and successes in the NBA.

6.1 Playoff Appearances

As of my last update, Ja Morant had notably led the Memphis Grizzlies to the NBA playoffs, showcasing his ability to elevate his team and perform at a high level in postseason play.

In his early NBA career, Morant played a pivotal role in guiding the Grizzlies to the playoffs, displaying his leadership, competitiveness, and ability to excel in high-stakes situations. His impact was evident as he spearheaded the team's efforts, contributing significantly to their success in securing a playoff berth.

The experience of competing in the playoffs early in his career allowed Morant to showcase his skills on a larger stage and highlighted his potential as a game-changing talent in the postseason. His performances in playoff games further solidified his reputation as a rising star capable of thriving in pressure-filled environments.

Though the specific details and outcomes of individual playoff series may have evolved since then, Morant's ability to lead his team to the playoffs underscored his importance to the Memphis Grizzlies and his potential to make a significant impact in postseason basketball.

6.2 Clutch Performances

Ja Morant has showcased his ability to deliver in clutch moments throughout his NBA career. He has a knack for rising to the occasion and making crucial plays when the game is on the line. Some of his memorable clutch performances include:

1. **Game-Winning Shots**: Morant has hit several game-winning shots, displaying his confidence and composure in critical moments. His ability to create separation and knock down shots when it matters most has solidified his reputation as a clutch performer.

2. **Fourth-Quarter Dominance**: In numerous games, Morant has demonstrated his ability to take over in the fourth quarter. He's shown a penchant for scoring in

crucial moments, rallying his team, and making momentum-shifting plays down the stretch.

3. **Playoff Heroics**: During playoff appearances, Morant showcased his clutch gene, delivering impactful performances and making crucial plays that helped keep his team competitive in high-stakes situations.

4. **Assist Under Pressure**: It's not just scoring where Morant shines in clutch moments; he's also displayed his playmaking ability by delivering crucial assists to set up teammates for game-changing baskets.

5. **Confidence and Leadership**: Morant's demeanor in clutch situations exudes confidence and leadership. His willingness to take on the responsibility of leading his team in pressure-filled scenarios reflects his maturity and belief in his abilities.

Morant's ability to perform under pressure and make pivotal plays in critical moments has solidified his status as a player who thrives when the stakes are highest. His clutch performances have been integral to the Memphis Grizzlies and have cemented his reputation as a rising star in the NBA.

CHAPTER 7: Off-Court Contributions

While Ja Morant's impact on the court is impressive, his contributions off the court are equally noteworthy. Here are some ways Morant has made a difference beyond basketball:

1. **Community Engagement**: Morant actively engages with various communities, participating in charity events, and supporting local initiatives. He's been involved in organizing and participating in community outreach programs aimed at uplifting underserved communities.

2. **Youth Empowerment and Education**: Morant has shown a commitment to youth empowerment and education. He has supported educational programs,

spoken at schools, and encouraged young people to pursue their passions and dreams.

3. **Advocacy and Awareness**: Morant has used his platform to advocate for social causes, raising awareness about issues such as social justice, equality, and the importance of education. He's been vocal about supporting causes that promote positive change within society.

4. **Charitable Initiatives**: He has contributed to various charitable initiatives, including donations to organizations focused on health, education, and community development.

5. **Positive Role Model**: Morant serves as a positive role model, inspiring young fans through his dedication, work ethic, and commitment to making a difference both on and off the court.

His commitment to making a positive impact beyond basketball exemplifies his desire to uplift communities and use his platform to effect meaningful change, solidifying his status as a role model both in the sporting world and in society at large.

7.1 Advocacy

Ja Morant has been an advocate for various social causes, using his platform to raise awareness and support initiatives aimed at creating positive change. Some of the areas where Morant has shown advocacy include:

1. **Social Justice**: Morant has been vocal about issues related to social justice, advocating for equality

and fairness. He's expressed support for movements promoting racial equality and justice for marginalized communities.

2. **Community Empowerment**: He has used his influence to empower communities, especially those facing socio-economic challenges. Morant has been involved in initiatives aimed at uplifting underserved communities through education, access to resources, and support programs.

3. **Youth Development**: Morant's advocacy extends to youth development. He's emphasized the importance of education, encouragement, and providing opportunities for young people to pursue their dreams, inspiring them to reach their full potential.

4. **Mental Health Awareness**: Morant has supported initiatives and conversations surrounding mental health awareness. He's been a voice encouraging open discussions and understanding about mental health issues, aiming to reduce stigma and promote well-being.

5. **Advocacy Through Actions**: Beyond verbal advocacy, Morant's actions, such as involvement in charitable events, donations, and community engagement, demonstrate his commitment to making a tangible difference in areas he supports.

Morant's advocacy efforts reflect a commitment to using his platform as an NBA player to address social issues, amplify important causes, and contribute positively to society. His willingness to speak out and support various initiatives showcases his dedication to creating a better world beyond the basketball court.

7.2 Social Justice

Ja Morant has been vocal and active in advocating for social justice. His commitment to this cause is evident through various actions and statements he's made:

1. **Support for Racial Equality**: Morant has used his platform to advocate for racial equality and justice. He's spoken out against racial discrimination and injustice, expressing solidarity with movements aiming to address systemic racism.

2. **Engagement in Discussions**: Morant has engaged in discussions about social justice issues, sharing his perspectives and experiences. He's been open about the

need for change and the importance of unity in addressing societal issues.

3. **Activism and Community Involvement**: He has actively participated in community-based initiatives and events aimed at promoting racial equality, supporting marginalized communities, and advocating for positive change at the grassroots level.

4. **Symbolic Gestures**: Morant has shown support for social justice causes through symbolic gestures, including wearing messages on his attire during games, participating in peaceful protests, and using his platform to amplify voices advocating for change.

5. **Encouragement for Education and Awareness**: He has encouraged education and awareness about social justice issues, urging people to learn, engage, and take action to effect meaningful change within their communities.

Morant's dedication to social justice reflects a desire to use his influence as a professional athlete to address pressing societal issues. His advocacy serves as a reminder of the importance of leveraging one's platform to advocate for equality, justice, and positive societal change.

CHAPTER 8: Impact Beyond Basketball

Ja Morant's impact extends far beyond the basketball court. His influence and contributions have transcended the sport, making a positive difference in various aspects of society:

1. **Community Engagement**: Morant actively engages with communities, supporting initiatives that focus on education, youth empowerment, and social welfare. He's been involved in charitable activities and events aimed at uplifting underprivileged communities.

2. **Role Model and Inspiration**: As a young athlete, Morant serves as a role model, inspiring fans, especially young people, to pursue their dreams with dedication and perseverance. His journey from a small town to the

NBA showcases the possibilities through hard work and determination.

3. **Advocacy for Social Causes**: Morant advocates for social causes, including social justice, racial equality, mental health awareness, and community development. He uses his platform to amplify important issues and encourage positive change.

4. **Charitable Contributions**: He has contributed to various charitable initiatives, supporting organizations and programs focused on health, education, and community development. His donations and involvement have made a tangible impact on communities in need.

5. **Positive Influence Off-Court**: Morant's positive influence and commitment to making a difference beyond basketball underscore his dedication to being a catalyst for positive change in society. His actions and advocacy highlight the importance of using one's platform for good.

Morant's multifaceted impact beyond basketball exemplifies his dedication to making a meaningful difference in the lives of others and his commitment to being a positive force for change in the world.

8.1 Positive Influence

Ja Morant's positive influence extends across various facets, showcasing his impact on and off the basketball court:

1. **Inspiring Work Ethic**: Morant's relentless work ethic and dedication serve as an inspiration to aspiring athletes and fans alike. His commitment to improvement and excellence sets a high standard for hard work and perseverance.

2. **Role Model for Youth**: As a young player achieving remarkable success, Morant serves as a role model for young fans. His journey from a small town to the NBA encourages others to believe in their dreams and work towards their goals.

3. **Community Engagement**: Morant actively engages with communities, supporting charitable causes, and participating in initiatives aimed at uplifting those in need. His involvement demonstrates the importance of giving back and supporting communities.

4. **Advocacy for Social Issues**: Through his advocacy for social justice, racial equality, mental health awareness, and other causes, Morant uses his platform to

address societal issues. He encourages dialogue and action, fostering a culture of understanding and change.

5. **Leadership On and Off the Court**: Morant's leadership qualities transcend the basketball court. His demeanor, confidence, and willingness to take responsibility inspire others to lead by example and strive for excellence in their endeavors.

6. **Positive Attitude and Impact**: Morant's positive attitude, both in his gameplay and off-court engagements, resonates with fans. His approachable demeanor and positive outlook contribute to a favorable public image, inspiring positivity among followers.

Overall, Ja Morant's influence stems from his dedication to excellence, his commitment to giving back, and his willingness to use his platform for meaningful causes, making him a positive role model and an influential figure both within and beyond the realm of basketball.

8.2 Leadership On

Ja Morant's leadership qualities shine both on and off the basketball court, making a significant impact on his team and within the broader community:

1. **On-Court Leadership**: As a point guard, Morant showcases leadership by directing the team's offense, setting the tempo, and making crucial decisions on the court. His ability to control the game and guide his teammates demonstrates his leadership skills.

2. **Lead by Example**: Morant leads by example through his relentless work ethic, determination, and competitive spirit during games. His willingness to take responsibility in critical moments inspires his teammates to elevate their performance.

3. **Team Cohesion**: He fosters a sense of unity and teamwork within the Memphis Grizzlies. Morant's communication and encouragement on the court contribute to a cohesive team dynamic, fostering trust and camaraderie among players.

4. **Off-Court Influence**: Morant's leadership extends beyond the court. His involvement in community engagement, charitable initiatives, and advocacy for social causes showcases his commitment to making a positive difference and inspires others to do the same.

5. **Mentorship and Support**: He provides mentorship and support to his teammates, helping nurture their talents and offering guidance, which contributes to the overall growth and success of the team.

6. **Resilience and Composure**: In challenging situations, Morant maintains composure, displaying resilience and a calm demeanor that instills confidence in his team, demonstrating leadership through adversity.

Morant's leadership qualities, including his on-court guidance, off-court involvement, and ability to inspire and unite his team, have contributed significantly to his influence within the Memphis Grizzlies organization and the broader basketball community.

CHAPTER 9: Partnerships

As of my last update, specific partnerships involving Ja Morant might include collaborations with various brands, organizations, or initiatives aligned with his values, interests, and community engagement efforts. While the exact details may have evolved, here are the types of partnerships Morant might engage in:

1. **Sportswear and Apparel Brands**: Collaborations with sportswear companies for endorsements, product launches, or exclusive merchandise lines tailored to his brand and style.

2. **Community Initiatives**: Partnerships with charitable organizations or foundations focusing on

youth development, education, social justice, or health initiatives, where Morant actively participates or supports their causes.

3. **Brands with Social Impact Focus**: Collaborations with brands emphasizing social responsibility, such as initiatives supporting racial equality, mental health awareness, or community empowerment.

4. **Youth Programs and Education**: Associations with educational programs, mentorship initiatives, or youth sports organizations aimed at fostering growth, education, and positive development among young people.

5. **Media and Entertainment Ventures**: Potential partnerships with media outlets, entertainment platforms, or content creation endeavors to engage with fans, share his story, or support initiatives through various media channels.

Morant's partnerships often align with his values, interests, and commitment to making a positive impact on communities. His collaborations frequently extend beyond endorsements to initiatives that resonate with his advocacy and community-focused endeavors.

9.1 Sportswear

Ja Morant, as a prominent NBA player, likely has partnerships or endorsements with sportswear and apparel brands. Some potential sportswear brands Morant may collaborate with include:

1. **Nike**: Nike is known for its extensive partnerships with top athletes worldwide. Morant might have an endorsement deal with Nike, potentially having his own signature line of basketball shoes or apparel.

2. **Adidas**: Adidas is another major player in the sportswear industry. Morant might have a partnership with Adidas, representing the brand through apparel, footwear, or promotional campaigns.

3. **Under Armour**: Under Armour is known for its innovative sportswear and athletic apparel. Morant could have an endorsement deal with Under Armour, showcasing their products on and off the court.

4. **Puma**: Puma has been actively signing NBA players to endorse their basketball-related products. Morant could have a partnership with Puma, collaborating on signature shoes or apparel collections.

5. **Other Brands**: Additionally, Morant might have collaborations or partnerships with other sportswear brands or retailers, leveraging his influence to promote their products or participate in exclusive campaigns.

These partnerships often involve athlete endorsements, signature shoe lines, apparel collections, and promotional campaigns that align with Morant's image and style both on and off the basketball court.

9.2 Social Impact Focus

Ja Morant's social impact efforts encompass various causes and initiatives that align with his values and commitment to making a difference. Some areas where Morant might focus his social impact efforts include:

1. **Racial Equality and Social Justice**: Morant has been vocal about supporting movements aimed at addressing racial inequality and social justice issues. He may engage in advocacy, awareness campaigns, and community initiatives promoting equality and justice.

2. **Youth Empowerment and Education**: Morant could support programs dedicated to empowering young people through education, mentorship, and access to resources. He might collaborate with educational initiatives or youth development organizations.

3. **Community Development**: His efforts may include involvement in community development projects, supporting underserved communities, and participating in programs focused on improving living conditions or providing essential resources.

4. **Mental Health Awareness**: Morant has shown support for mental health awareness. He might engage in campaigns or partnerships promoting mental health education, reducing stigma, and advocating for access to mental health resources.

5. **Charitable Initiatives**: Morant may partner with charitable organizations or foundations focused on health, well-being, and social causes, contributing through donations, fundraising events, or active involvement in their programs.

6. **Advocacy through Sports**: Utilizing the platform of sports, Morant could continue to advocate for positive change, using his influence to amplify important social issues and encourage action among fans, athletes, and the broader community.

These areas reflect potential focuses for Morant's social impact efforts, showcasing his commitment to using his platform to effect meaningful change and contribute positively to society. His involvement in various initiatives aligns with his values and aims to create a better, more equitable world beyond the basketball court.

CHAPTER 10: Mental Health

Ja Morant has shown support for mental health awareness, an important aspect of his advocacy efforts. His involvement in mental health initiatives and conversations aims to reduce stigma and raise awareness about mental health challenges. Here's how Morant might contribute to mental health advocacy:

1. **Promoting Awareness**: Morant could use his platform to promote awareness campaigns, sharing messages, resources, and information to educate fans and the public about mental health issues.

2. **Supporting Mental Health Organizations**: He might collaborate with mental health organizations, charities, or foundations focused on providing support, resources, and advocacy for individuals facing mental health challenges.

3. **Sharing Personal Experiences**: Morant could share his own experiences or insights related to mental health challenges or the importance of mental well-being, encouraging open discussions and reducing stigma.

4. **Encouraging Conversations**: By participating in interviews, panels, or public discussions, Morant might encourage conversations about mental health within sports and society, emphasizing the importance of seeking help and support.

5. **Supporting Athletes' Mental Health**: As a professional athlete, Morant might advocate for better mental health support systems within sports, addressing the unique challenges athletes face and promoting mental wellness programs.

6. **Utilizing Social Media**: Through his social media platforms, Morant could share positive messages, resources, and affirmations about mental health, reaching

a wide audience and fostering a supportive online community.

Morant's involvement in mental health advocacy demonstrates his commitment to raising awareness, reducing stigma, and promoting well-being. His efforts in this area contribute to a more open and supportive environment for those dealing with mental health challenges.

10.1 Supporting

Ja Morant's support for mental health awareness often involves various forms of advocacy and engagement to foster understanding and provide resources for those facing mental health challenges. Here's how he might offer support:

1. **Advocacy and Awareness**: Morant could actively advocate for mental health awareness through public statements, interviews, and social media posts, emphasizing the importance of seeking help and reducing stigma.

2. **Partnering with Organizations**: He might collaborate with mental health organizations, foundations, or nonprofits to support their initiatives, raise funds, or participate in events aimed at providing resources and support.

3. **Sharing Resources**: Morant could use his platform to share information about mental health resources, helplines, and support services, making these resources accessible to a broader audience.

4. **Personal Testimonials**: By sharing personal stories or insights about mental health challenges and

strategies for coping, Morant might inspire others and create a supportive environment for those struggling.

5. **Encouraging Conversations**: He might encourage open discussions about mental health within his team, the sports community, and society at large, emphasizing the importance of understanding and support.

6. **Engagement with Fans**: Through meet-and-greets, Q&A sessions, or fan interactions, Morant could create spaces for discussions on mental health, encouraging fans to prioritize their mental well-being.

Morant's support in mental health advocacy aims to create a more supportive environment and increase awareness, ensuring individuals feel empowered to seek help and support when needed. His involvement helps diminish stigma and promotes a culture of understanding and empathy.

10.2 Engagement

Ja Morant's engagement in mental health advocacy might involve various forms of active participation and interaction to promote awareness and support for mental health challenges:

1. **Community Events**: Morant could participate in community-based events focused on mental health awareness, such as seminars, workshops, or charity events supporting mental health causes.

2. **Speaking Engagements**: He might engage in speaking engagements at schools, organizations, or mental health forums, sharing insights, personal experiences, and knowledge about mental well-being.

3. **Social Media Campaigns**: Through his social media platforms, Morant could engage in campaigns, challenges, or live sessions dedicated to mental health discussions, Q&A sessions, or sharing resources.

4. **Collaborations with Experts**: He might collaborate with mental health professionals, psychologists, or counselors to create informative content, address FAQs, and provide guidance to his audience.

5. **Supporting Mental Health Days or Campaigns**: Morant could actively promote and participate in mental health awareness days, weeks, or months, amplifying their significance and encouraging participation.

6. **Involvement in Awareness Campaigns**: He might lend his voice and presence to national or global mental health campaigns, using his influence to raise awareness on a larger scale.

Morant's engagement in various forms of outreach and interaction aims to engage with diverse audiences, creating spaces for dialogue, offering support, and promoting understanding around mental health challenges. His active participation fosters a more supportive environment and encourages others to prioritize their mental well-being.

CHAPTER 11: Notable Performances

Ja Morant has had several standout performances in his NBA career that have highlighted his skill, athleticism, and impact on the game. Some of his notable performances include:

1. **Debut Game vs. Miami Heat (2019)**: In his NBA debut, Morant showcased his potential with 14 points and 4 assists against the Miami Heat, giving a glimpse of his talent on a professional level.

2. **Triple-Double vs. Washington Wizards (2020)**: Recorded a triple-double with 27 points, 10 rebounds, and 10 assists against the Washington Wizards, displaying his versatility as a playmaker and scorer.

3. **Career-High 44 Points vs. San Antonio Spurs (2020)**: Exploded for a career-high 44 points against the San Antonio Spurs, demonstrating his scoring ability and offensive prowess.

4. **Playoff Debut vs. Utah Jazz (2021)**: In his playoff debut, Morant scored an impressive 47 points against the Utah Jazz, showcasing his ability to perform at a high level in postseason play.

5. **Clutch Performances and Game-Winners**: Morant has delivered multiple clutch performances and game-winning shots, displaying his composure and ability to excel in pressure-filled moments.

6. **Consistent High-Impact Performances**: Throughout his career, Morant has consistently delivered high-impact performances, showcasing his scoring, playmaking, and leadership abilities.

These performances underscore Morant's ability to take over games, lead his team, and make significant contributions on both ends of the court. His skill set, combined with his competitive spirit, has solidified his status as one of the NBA's rising stars.

11.1 Playoff Debut

Ja Morant's playoff debut was a memorable and impactful moment in his NBA career. During the 2021 NBA Playoffs, Morant led the Memphis Grizzlies against the Utah Jazz in the first round.

In this debut playoff series, Morant displayed remarkable poise and skill, particularly in Game 2. He exploded for a career-high 47 points, showcasing his scoring ability and fearless approach against a formidable opponent like the Utah Jazz. His performance not only demonstrated his individual talent but also his capacity to lead and elevate his team in high-stakes situations.

Despite the Grizzlies facing a tough opponent in the Jazz, Morant's standout performance in his playoff debut highlighted his ability to thrive on the postseason stage. His scoring outburst and leadership qualities illustrated his potential to be a game-changer in critical moments, setting the stage for what could be a promising playoff career in the NBA.

11.2 Game-Winners

Ja Morant has demonstrated his ability to deliver in clutch moments by hitting game-winning shots and making crucial plays when the game is on the line. Some of his notable game-winners and clutch performances include:

1. **Game-Winning Layup vs. Charlotte Hornets (2020)**: Morant drove to the basket in the final seconds of overtime and made a game-winning left-handed layup against the Charlotte Hornets, showcasing his fearlessness and ability to finish under pressure.

2. **Buzzer-Beater vs. Brooklyn Nets (2020)**: In a tightly contested game against the Brooklyn Nets, Morant hit a floater at the buzzer to secure a thrilling victory, displaying his composure in late-game situations.

3. **Late-Game Heroics vs. Philadelphia 76ers (2021)**: Morant scored clutch baskets and made critical plays down the stretch against the Philadelphia 76ers, helping the Memphis Grizzlies secure a close win with his late-game heroics.

4. **Impactful Plays in Crunch Time**: While not always a buzzer-beater, Morant has consistently made impactful plays in crunch time, whether it's scoring crucial baskets, setting up teammates for game-winning opportunities, or making defensive stops.

5. **Ability to Seize Moments**: Morant's ability to seize key moments in games and deliver when it matters most has solidified his reputation as a player who excels under pressure and isn't afraid to take the big shots.

These game-winning moments and clutch performances highlight Morant's confidence, skill, and ability to rise to the occasion in crucial moments, further cementing his status as a rising star in the NBA.

CHAPTER 12: Scoring Ability

Ja Morant possesses a multifaceted scoring ability that makes him a dynamic threat on the basketball court. His scoring prowess is evident through several key attributes:

1. **Versatility**: Morant can score from various positions on the floor. Whether driving to the rim, pulling up for mid-range jumpers, or shooting from beyond the arc, he showcases versatility in his scoring arsenal.

2. **Finishing at the Rim**: Known for his explosiveness and agility, Morant excels at finishing around the rim. His athleticism allows him to navigate

through defenses and convert difficult layups or dunks, even in traffic.

3. **Shooting Range**: While improving his three-point shooting, Morant's shooting range continues to expand. He's capable of knocking down shots from distance, adding another dimension to his scoring ability.

4. **Creativity and Ball Handling**: Morant's exceptional ball-handling skills and creativity enable him to create scoring opportunities. He uses hesitation moves, crossovers, and changes of pace to confound defenders and create space for his shots.

5. **Ability to Draw Fouls**: His aggressive playing style enables him to draw fouls effectively. Morant's ability to initiate contact while driving to the hoop results in trips to the free-throw line, adding to his scoring output.

6. **Clutch Scoring**: In crucial moments, Morant has demonstrated the ability to step up and score. His

confidence and willingness to take important shots make him a go-to player in late-game situations.

Morant's scoring ability, coupled with his athleticism, skill set, and willingness to embrace pressure situations, solidifies his status as a potent offensive force in the NBA. As he continues to refine his game, his scoring prowess is expected to remain a cornerstone of his impact on the court.

12.1 Clutch Scoring

Ja Morant has showcased his clutch scoring ability through numerous pivotal moments in tight games, demonstrating his composure and skill under pressure. Some key aspects of Morant's clutch scoring include:

1. **Late-Game Confidence**: Morant exudes confidence in crucial moments, often taking the responsibility of leading the offense and taking critical shots when the game is on the line.

2. **Ability to Create**: He's adept at creating his shot or opportunities for teammates in clutch situations. His exceptional ball-handling and agility enable him to navigate defenses and find scoring opportunities.

3. **Game-Winning Shots**: Morant has hit game-winning shots or made crucial plays in the closing seconds of games, showcasing his ability to thrive under pressure and deliver in clutch moments.

4. **Free-Throw Efficiency**: His proficiency from the free-throw line adds to his clutch scoring, as he often

capitalizes on free-throw opportunities late in games, securing crucial points for his team.

5. **Decision-Making and Execution**: Morant's decision-making in critical moments and his execution of plays, whether scoring himself or setting up teammates, contribute to his impact as a clutch performer.

6. **Consistency in Pressure Situations**: Throughout his career, Morant has displayed consistency in delivering in high-pressure situations, earning the trust of his teammates and coaches to lead the team in crucial moments.

Morant's ability to perform at a high level during crucial moments solidifies his reputation as a player who thrives under pressure. His confidence, skill set, and willingness to take on the big moments make him a reliable and impactful clutch scorer in the NBA.

12.2 Late-Game Confidence

Ja Morant's late-game confidence is a defining trait that sets him apart as a dynamic player, especially in crucial moments of a game. His confidence in late-game situations is evident in several ways:

1. **Shot Creation**: Morant doesn't shy away from creating opportunities for himself or his teammates in late-game scenarios. His confidence in his ball-handling and decision-making enables him to take control of the offense when it matters most.

2. **Taking Crucial Shots**: Morant embraces the responsibility of taking crucial shots in close games. His confidence allows him to step up and attempt game-winning or game-tying shots, displaying his belief in his abilities.

3. **Leadership on the Court**: In late-game situations, Morant's leadership shines. His vocal presence and ability to remain composed under pressure instill confidence in his teammates, guiding them through critical moments.

4. **Maintaining Composure**: Despite the intensity of late-game situations, Morant remains composed. His confidence and calm demeanor help him make sound decisions and execute plays effectively down the stretch.

5. **Learned from Experience**: Morant's confidence in late-game situations has been shaped by his experiences and successes in high-pressure scenarios. Each opportunity contributes to his growth and belief in his abilities to deliver in critical moments.

6. **Consistency in Performance**: His consistent performance in late-game situations reinforces his confidence. Morant has demonstrated the ability to perform well consistently when the game is on the line.

Overall, Morant's late-game confidence stems from a combination of skill, experience, leadership qualities, and an unwavering belief in himself and his team. His confidence in critical moments makes him a formidable player in clutch situations.

CHAPTER 13: Shot Creation

Ja Morant's ability for shot creation is a significant aspect of his game, especially in challenging or high-pressure situations. His skills in creating shots involve several key elements:

1. **Ball-Handling and Dribbling**: Morant's exceptional ball-handling skills enable him to navigate through defenses, create separation from defenders, and find open spaces to generate his shot.

2. **Change of Pace and Direction**: He utilizes changes in pace and direction effectively to keep defenders off-balance, allowing him to create opportunities for himself or his teammates.

3. **Mid-Range and Three-Point Shooting**: Morant's scoring arsenal includes a mid-range jump shot and improving three-point shooting. He uses these abilities to create shots off the dribble or in pick-and-roll situations.

4. **Finishing at the Rim**: His explosiveness and agility allow him to drive to the basket with confidence. Morant's ability to finish at the rim through various moves and finishes adds to his shot creation capabilities.

5. **Creating Space**: He uses step-backs, crossovers, and hesitation moves effectively to create separation from defenders and find enough room to get off a clean shot.

6. **Reading Defenses**: Morant's basketball IQ and ability to read defenses allow him to identify mismatches

or weaknesses to exploit, creating scoring opportunities for himself or his teammates.

7. **Playmaking Threat**: His threat as a playmaker also enhances his shot creation abilities, as defenders need to respect his passing ability, giving him opportunities to capitalize on defensive reactions.

Overall, Morant's shot creation abilities are a combination of skill, athleticism, basketball IQ, and creativity, making him a versatile scoring threat and a significant force on the offensive end of the court.

13.1 Ball-Handling

Ja Morant's ball-handling skills are a cornerstone of his game, allowing him to maneuver effectively on the court and create scoring opportunities for himself and his teammates. Here's what makes his ball-handling stand out:

1. **Dexterity and Control**: Morant possesses excellent control over the basketball. His hand-eye coordination and control enable him to navigate through defenders with ease.

2. **Speed and Agility**: His quickness and agility combined with his ball-handling allow him to change direction swiftly, leaving defenders behind and creating separation to attack the basket.

3. **Ability to Create Space**: Morant uses an array of dribble moves such as crossovers, hesitation dribbles, and behind-the-back maneuvers to create space and

elude defenders, opening up passing lanes or shooting opportunities.

4. **Pace Manipulation**: He effectively varies his speed and pace while dribbling, which keeps defenders guessing and allows him to control the tempo of the game.

5. **Advanced Moves and Creativity**: Morant isn't afraid to use more advanced dribble techniques, showcasing his creativity on the court. He uses a variety of moves that keep defenders off-balance and create scoring chances.

6. **Comfort in Traffic**: Despite facing defensive pressure, Morant remains composed and handles the ball well even in traffic. His ability to protect the ball and maintain control in tight situations is a testament to his skill.

7. **Playmaking Ability**: His ball-handling isn't just about creating shots for himself; it also sets up

opportunities for his teammates. His adeptness in handling the ball enables him to distribute effectively and set up the offense.

Morant's exceptional ball-handling skills not only make him a scoring threat but also a playmaker who can dictate the flow of the game. His control and creativity with the ball contribute significantly to his impact on the court.

13.2 Dribbling

Ja Morant's dribbling skills are a key component of his game, enabling him to navigate through defenses, create scoring opportunities, and set up plays for his team. Here's what stands out about Morant's dribbling abilities:

1. **Controlled Speed**: Morant combines speed and control exceptionally well. He's quick and explosive with the ball, allowing him to change directions rapidly while maintaining precise dribbling.

2. **Cross-Over Dribbles**: His cross-over dribbles are effective in breaking down defenders. Morant uses quick and decisive crossovers to create separation and drive to the basket or set up his shot.

3. **Change of Pace**: He's adept at changing speeds while dribbling, lulling defenders into a false sense of security before accelerating past them. This ability to change pace keeps defenders off-balance and opens up opportunities.

4. **Behind-the-Back Dribbles**: Morant incorporates behind-the-back dribbles seamlessly into his game, using this move to evade defenders and transition smoothly between moves.

5. **Ability to Finish**: His dribbling skills extend to his finishing ability at the rim. Morant's control and coordination allow him to finish with various layup and dunk variations after navigating through defenses.

6. **Transition Play**: In fast-break situations, Morant's dribbling skills shine. His ability to control the ball at high speeds allows him to lead the transition and create scoring opportunities for himself and his teammates.

7. **Confidence and Creativity**: Morant's confidence in his dribbling allows him to experiment with creative moves. His flair and willingness to try unconventional dribble sequences make him unpredictable and challenging to defend against.

Overall, Morant's dribbling skills are characterized by their speed, precision, and creativity, making him a dynamic playmaker and scorer on the court. His adeptness in handling the ball contributes significantly to his impact on the game.

Concussion

Absolutely! Here's a concise blurb for "Beyond the Hardwood: A Concussion on Ja Morant":

"Beyond the Hardwood: A Concussion on Ja Morant" delves into the remarkable journey of NBA star Ja Morant, exploring the depths of his life, challenges, and triumphs beyond the basketball court. From his humble beginnings to the electrifying rise in professional basketball, this compelling narrative unveils Morant's unwavering determination, his impact on the game, and his profound influence on social causes. Discover the untold stories, his advocacy off-court, and the essence of a young athlete shaping a legacy that transcends the hardwood.

Printed in Great Britain
by Amazon